THE GREAT HORNED OWL

BY
LYNN M. STONE

EDITED BY
DR. HOWARD SCHROEDER
Professor in Reading and Language Arts
Dept. of Elementary Education
Mankato State University

PRODUCED AND DESIGNED BY
BAKER STREET PRODUCTIONS
Mankato, MN

CRESTWOOD HOUSE
Mankato, Minnesota

CIP

LIBRARY OF CONGRESS CATALOGING IN PUBLICATION DATA

Stone, Lynn M.
  The great horned owl.

  (Wildlife, habits & habitat)
  SUMMARY: Examines the physical characteristics, habitat, life cycle, and behavior of the owl who bears the nickname, "winged tiger."
  1. Great horned owl--Juvenile literature. (1. Great horned owl. 2. Owls.) I. Schroeder, Howard. II. Baker Street Productions. III. Title. IV. Series.
QL696.S83S76   1987   598'.97   87-570
ISBN 0-89686-325-5

International Standard Book Number:	Library of Congress Catalog Card Number:
Library Binding 0-89686-325-5	87-570

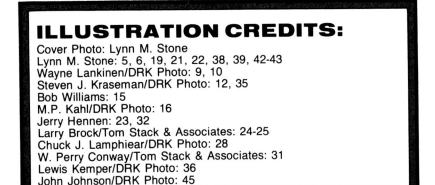

ILLUSTRATION CREDITS:

Cover Photo: Lynn M. Stone
Lynn M. Stone: 5, 6, 19, 21, 22, 38, 39, 42-43
Wayne Lankinen/DRK Photo: 9, 10
Steven J. Kraseman/DRK Photo: 12, 35
Bob Williams: 15
M.P. Kahl/DRK Photo: 16
Jerry Hennen: 23, 32
Larry Brock/Tom Stack & Associates: 24-25
Chuck J. Lamphiear/DRK Photo: 28
W. Perry Conway/Tom Stack & Associates: 31
Lewis Kemper/DRK Photo: 36
John Johnson/DRK Photo: 45

CRESTWOOD HOUSE

Hwy. 66 South, Box 3427
Mankato, MN 56002-3427

TABLE OF CONTENTS

INTRODUCTION:

People have looked carefully at owls for a long time. The first drawing of a bird has been identified as an owl. The artist lived during the Stone Age, thousands of years ago.

Our ancestors had many different ideas about owls. The Tlingit Indians of Alaska thought owls were "big medicine." The medicine man kept parts of owls as symbols of power. Tlingit children were taught that an owl would take them away if they cried too much. Tlingit adults believed that owls "told" bad news.

The Koyukon Athapaskan Indians of Alaska believed that owls were wise. The great horned owl, the topic of this book, was the wisest of all owls. These Indians said great horned owls brought messages. The Indians believed that the owls sometimes told them, "Soon you will cry." That meant that someone close to them was going to die. If the owl told them, "You will eat the belly of something," it meant that food was near.

Hundreds of years ago, the Greek people connected owls with their gods of wisdom. But other people thought the owl was a sign of evil, and still others thought owls could help them avoid evil. Owl wings nailed to a barn were supposed to turn away bad luck. Owl broth or soup was supposed to be a cure for children's diseases.

The owl that most of us think of when any owl comes

The great horned owl is one of the most recognized of all owls.

to mind is the great horned owl. It is the owl we are most likely to see. No wonder. It can live almost anywhere it finds trees, and in a few places where trees are very scarce. Its home range includes the entire United States except Hawaii, most of Canada, central America, and almost all of South America. In Europe and Asia the great horned owl has a close cousin, the eagle owl, the largest owl in the world.

Great horned owls are certainly the best known owls in North America. They look the way that owls are "supposed" to look. They have big, golden eyes and ear tufts like a cat. They sit upright and look wise and alert. Yet their fame comes from their bravery as well as their looks. No other bird their size is any fiercer, stronger, or more fearless. No other bird has earned the name "winged tiger."

The great horned owl is a very special bird—not a wise bird, mind you, but a bird of great interest to us.

The great horned owl, sometimes called "winged tiger," is known for its bravery and strength.

CHAPTER ONE:

The great horned owl's closest kin

The great horned owl is only one of many kinds of owls. Named *Bubo virginianus* by ornithologists, the scientists who study birds, the great horned owl belongs to a large group of birds called *strigiformes*. Except to ornithologists, the *strigiformes* are commonly known as owls.

The great horned owl is one of about one hundred and thirty kinds of owls found throughout the world. The only large land area of the world without owls is Antarctica. In North America, *Bubo* is one of eighteen owl species or kinds.

As a separate species of owls, the great horned owl is, in some ways, different from its owl cousins. But at the same time, it shares many features with other owls. All owls have large, rounded heads with forward-facing eyes. There is a "ruff" of feathers around the eyes. This ruff is called the facial disk. The facial disks help give the owl a look of surprise or wonder.

The owls' beaks are short, very sharp, and hooked. Along with that powerful beak, owls have very strong claws or talons at the ends of their toes. As one might expect of a bird with such weapons, owls can swoop down and catch other animals for their meals.

Owls have excellent eyesight, even in poor light. They also hear very well, much better than people. Their wings are usually wide and rounded. Their tail feathers are fairly short and square. Female owls are almost always larger than their mates.

The great horned owl's closest relatives, other than owls, are the whippoorwill and its family of birds. You may have heard a whippoorwill at night. Its call sounds very much like its name—*whip-poor-will!*

Like an owl, the whippoorwill hunts late in the day and in darkness. These birds do not have hooked bills or talons, but they do have fluffy, soft feathers similar to the owl's.

Eagles and hawks are not as closely related to owls as people once believed. Like the owls, the eagle family has sharp beaks and talons, and they catch prey (other animals) for food. But eagles and hawks are diurnal; they are birds of the daylight hours. Most owls are nocturnal; they hunt at night. Hawks and eagles do not have the forward-facing eyes or the loose, fluffy feathers of owls either. Owls often swallow their small prey whole. Hawks and eagles tear their prey into pieces. Owls, like parrots, use their feet to lift food to their mouths. The hawks and eagles lower their heads to their talons.

Recognizing the great horned owl

Among the owls of North America, the great horned owl is not hard to identify. *Bubo* measures from eighteen to twenty-five inches (46 - 64 cm) from tip of bill to tip of tail. It has a wingspread of thirty-five to fifty-five inches (90 - 141 cm). This weight makes the great horned owl a heavyweight among American owls, and the female is more of a heavyweight than the male. Ornithologists are not sure why female owls are larger. A possible reason is that the female can better defend herself and her young against a fierce male if she is bigger. In most species of hawks the female is also larger than the male.

The great horned owl is the largest American owl with ear tufts. The other "tufted" owls are much smaller.

The great horned owl is the largest of the "tufted" owls.

The whiskered owl is six and one-half inches (17 cm) long. The screech owl stands just eight inches (20.5 cm) tall. The long-eared owl looks much like the great horned, but it is smaller than a crow.

The "earless" great gray owl of the North seems to be the biggest North American owl. The great gray owl, which lives in evergreen forests, can be thirty-three inches (84.5 cm) long, but much of its bulk is made up of extra feathers. In fact, many great horned owls are heavier than the great gray owl. Great horned owls weigh from three to five pounds (1.4 - 2.3 kg). The heaviest North American owl is the snowy, which can weigh up

The heaviest owl of North America is the snowy owl.

to six pounds (2.7 kg). The largest great horned owls live in the Far North of Canada and Alaska and in the Andes Mountains of Ecuador. The smallest are found in Central America and Mexico.

The great horned owl's ear tufts are really feathers. The owl raises the two-inch tufts on both sides of its head at will. Of course, the tufts do look like ears, so they have earned the great horned owl the nickname "cat owl." The tufts look like "horns," too, and the bird's scientific name, *Bubo*, means "horned owl" in the Latin language. The feathered tufts are somewhat of a mystery. But they seem to be used to let other owls know one another's moods. An angry or startled owl, for instance, raises its ear tufts. Among such fierce birds, it is important to avoid trouble with one another. The use of the ear tufts may help them do just that.

Great horned owls have a white throat or bib. Otherwise, they are often dressed in browns and grays with some black bars across their chests. The disks around the yellow eyes are reddish-brown. Males and females wear the same colors. The great horned owl's plumage (its entire clothing of feathers) is ideal for helping it hide in woodlands.

Great horned owls wear similar plumage, but they are not exactly alike. Their plumage depends on the area in which they live. Like other kinds of animals that live over a very large area, great horned owls look somewhat different from one part of North America to another. Because of these differences, ornithologists say there are several "races." Races are slightly different groups of the same basic animal. Each group has minor differences, usually in color or size, from the other groups. The great horned owls of the Far North, for example, have light-colored feathers. Some of these Arctic horned owls are almost as white as snowy owls. The dusky horned owls of the rainy Pacific coast are very dark.

There are several "races" of great horned owls. Some are lighter, such as this northern race, and some are darker.

Owl talk

The great horned owl, because it is more active at night than during the day, is more often heard than seen. One of the great horned owl's nicknames is "big hoot owl." True, the great horned owl "hoots," especially in late winter. But trying to identify the great horned owl by its voice can be hard to do. *Bubo*, it seems, has many voices!

Male great horned owls usually sound four or five booming hoots. Females usually sound six or eight hoots. The hoot sounds something like *oot-too-hoo, hoo-hoo*. It's one of the most exciting calls of the night. But great horned owls can also sound like foghorns, train whistles, and fighting tomcats. Even what sounds like the soft cooing of a dove in the forest may be a great horned owl.

Great horned owls often call back and forth to one another. They seem to have a system of communication by voice. So far, however, ornithologists understand very little about the owls' chatter with one another. For whatever reasons, great horned owls seem to be eager to hoot. They can easily be fooled by skillful human callers. Owls often hoot back to people who hoot to them in woodlands.

CHAPTER TWO:

A taste for meat

The great horned owl's "ears" and voice have earned it nicknames. Because as a hunter it is very strong, skillful, and fierce, it has still another nickname: winged tiger. Like the tiger, the great horned owl can survive only if it can attack and kill other animals. Great horned owls rarely dine on another animal's kill. They prefer fresh prey and will attack almost any smaller animal. Now and then a great horned owl attacks an animal larger than itself. The list of animals known to have been eaten by great horned owls is lengthy. Just a portion of that list includes rabbits, rats, gophers, mice, shrews, bats, flying squirrels, tree squirrels, woodchucks, skunks, fish weasels, domestic cats, Canada geese, grebes, small herons, sandpipers, ducks, woodpeckers, other owls, and even rattlesnakes. A captive great horned owl killed and ate part of another great horned owl which had been its mate for seven years.

Great horned owls sometimes catch insects, such as big crickets. But adult owls usually eat larger prey. Rabbits and mice are favorites. Every so often, the prey that the great horned owl hunts becomes plentiful. Then the owl may kill more prey than it really needs. When this happens, the owl may become quite fussy and, like some people, eat only the best pieces of flesh.

Squirrel

Rat

Bat

Rabbit

These are only a few of the many animals that the great horned owl preys on for food.

Tools of the hunter

Everything about the great horned owl helps it to be a master hunter. Its feathers, eyes, ears, beak, talons—even the way its bones are made—help the owl catch its prey.

The great horned owl's feathers help it fly silently. Not all birds, of course, do fly quietly. But the owl's feathers are different from the feathers of other birds. While a hawk's flight feathers are stiff, the long flight

The flight feathers well equip the great horned owl for its hunting.

16

feathers of the great horned owl have soft edges. The feathers on the wing surfaces are like velvet. All these feathers soften the noise made by the air rushing around them. The owl's feathers are its in-flight "muffler," just as the muffler on a car quiets engine noise.

The shape of the owl's wings helps to keep flight noise to a whisper. Its wings are huge for its body. The wide, rounded shape of the wings gives the great horned owl an unusual amount of "lift." The wings and the paper-thin, air-filled bones make the owl light in the air. With its great lift, the great horned owl does not have to "pump" its wings very much. The pumping of wings increases wind noise. Pheasants, for example, make a loud clattering noise when they take off from the ground. Goldeneye ducks' wings whistle when they fly.

For *Bubo*, the rule is silence. If the owl flew with a lot of noise, its prey would know the owl was attacking. More important, the great horned owl can locate its prey just by listening! A noisy flight would mean that the owl could no longer hear the sounds of the animal it was hunting. By flying silently, the great horned owl not only can hear its prey, but can surprise it, too.

The great horned owl's ears are no less than amazing! They can hear the squeak of a mouse one hundred yards away—the length of a football field. They also can hear a tiny animal rustling in the grass at the same distance.

In the early 1950's, two scientists showed how important the owl's ears are. Their barn owls easily caught mice in a completely dark room. But at first the scientists, Roger Payne and William Drury, were not sure how owls did this. They knew that owls could not see the mice. No animal can see in total darkness. The scientists played a tape recording of mice moving. The owls attacked the speaker playing the tape. The men then tied a ball of paper to the tail of a mouse. They released the mouse and its paper wad in a dark room. Walking on sand, the mouse itself did not make any noise, but the paper wad did. The owl attacked the paper.

The scientists showed that the barn owl found its prey by sound. If the owl had sensed body heat, it would have attacked the mouse. If it had used its sense of smell, it would have been able to attack the mouse instead of the paper. (Like most birds, owls do not appear to have a good sense of smell.)

More recently, scientists have shown that barn owls have a good memory for sounds. They can tell one sound from another. That skill helps the barn owl to identify what it should attack and what it should not attack. The great horned owl's ears may or may not be as keen as a barn owl's. Scientists do know that the great horned owl's ears are far more sensitive than ours.

The great horned owl's ears are deep, hidden slits on the sides of its head. The disks on the owl's face may help "cup" the sound toward the ears.

The eyes of a great horned owl look like little, yellow saucers. In fact, *Bubo's* eyes are the size of a human's. The great horned owl's eyes are so large that together

The eyes of the great horned owl are as large as human eyes and very powerful.

they are larger than its brain. If human eyes took up as much body space as the great horned owl's eyes, our eyes might be the size of real saucers.

The great horned owl's eyes are not only big, they are very powerful. While human eyes begin to fail in poor light, the owl's eyes still gather enough light to be useful. Just the moon and stars provide enough light for the great horned owl to be able to fly and hunt.

In some ways the great horned owl's eyes are like ours. Both of the owl's eyes face forward and both see the same scene. That type of vision, called binocular vision, helps the owl in judging distance. Like our eyes, the great horned owl's eyes do not make distant objects look larger than they are. But the owl does see distant objects more clearly than people can.

The great horned owl's eyes are not quite as good—or as bad—as many people think. Despite what most people believe, even owls cannot see in complete darkness. However, owls are not blind in daylight either. The great horned owl sees very well during the day, but it is a better hunter at night.

The great horned owl's eyes are fixed in bony sockets. The eyeballs do not move around, so it cannot see very much to either side. But it can easily move its head from side to side without having to move its body. The owl's neck is very flexible. People once believed that owls could turn their heads completely around—to the point of breaking their necks. An owl can turn its head halfway around very easily, and some species can turn three-quarters of a full circle! Owls, then, have the ability to turn their heads much farther than hawks or humans, but they do not turn a full circle. Turning its head helps the owl see over wide distances.

Owls appear more human-like than any other bird. Their eyes—and eyelids—have something to do with that. They are the only group of birds to drop an upper eyelid when they blink. People blink the same way. A sleepy owl raises its lower lid, as other birds do. A third eyelid, called the nictitans, is made of see-through skin. By blinking the nictitans, the owl can see, moisten its eyes, and protect its eyeball at the same time.

Owls are the only birds that drop an upper eyelid when they blink, just as humans do.

With its excellent hearing and eyesight, the great horned owl can usually find a meal. Often it sits quietly on a perch, waiting, and listening. When leaving its perch, the owl becomes a silent dive bomber, gliding toward its target. Just before it strikes, the great horned owl stretches its feet forward and tosses its head back. Each foot has four toes ending in needle-sharp talons about one-and-one-quarter inches (3 cm) long. The owl's curved talons spread widely apart and lock when they strike an animal. The force of the talons kills most prey instantly. The owl carries its kill in one foot. It rarely flies with food in its beak.

Not every strike means a fast kill. The owl may miss its target. If *Bubo* attacks an animal larger than it can

The needle-sharp talons of the great horned owl are about one-and-one-quarter inches (3 cm) long.

easily kill, it may fight or decide to fly away. Fighting with prey can result in injury or even death for the owl. A great horned owl that attacked a porcupine died with sixty-six quills in its body. Great horned owls usually are careful to attack only animals they can kill and carry. Hunger is probably the reason they sometimes tackle bigger prey.

Great horned owls swallow much of their prey whole. Several hours later, undigested bone and bits of fur are forced up from the owls' stomachs through their mouths. The fur and bone are pressed tightly together in pellets or castings about the size of a thumb. Scientists can tell what the owls have been eating from the kinds of bones in their pellets.

The pellets left by the great horned owl reveal food it has eaten.

A great horned owl catches one of its favorite foods, rabbit.

CHAPTER THREE:

Courtship and nest sites

Great horned owls do not spend all their time hunting. In the cold of winter they begin the activities that lead to nesting. Hooting among the owls increases as they begin to seek mates. At this time of year, the noisy owls may hoot throughout the night. But owl courtship is not just hooting. To attract a female, a male great horned owl may snap its bill, bow, and jump about. People who have watched the owls say the male's act, called a courtship display, looks like a dance.

By February the great horned owls are ready to raise a family. The first step is to find a nest. Great horned owls don't build nests of their own. They often take over a nest which another animal, usually a bird or squirrel, has already built in a tall tree. Great horned owls like the big, stick nests of crows, eagles, hawks, ospreys, and magpies. The owls may place a few twigs, weed stalks, roots, and feathers in the nest. Otherwise, the "borrowed" nest is just what they want.

Since the owls nest in winter, they rarely find the nest's original owners in it. If the nest builders happen to return, they find new owners—the owls. Rather than fight the fierce great horned owls, the nest builders usually go elsewhere. Great horned owls have even been known to chase eagles from their own nest.

Great horned owls are not choosy about their meals—nor about their nests. If the owls cannot find a stick nest, they will use a hole in a tree trunk, especially in the East. They also will lay eggs near the mouth of a cave or on a rocky ledge. Again, the great horned owls add nothing to the nest except for a few old bones, bits of fur, and feathers.

Because most birds nest in the spring, their nests are hidden by green leaves. As a winter nester, the great horned owl sits on a nest in the open. The owls even draw attention to their nests by the pellets that may collect below them.

The new eggs

Once they are settled in their nest, great horned owls usually lay two or three eggs. In the Arctic, where food may be very plentiful, great horned owls may lay six eggs. The eggs are the size of jumbo chicken eggs, but they are more round. The eggs are white and have a rough finish. Both the male and female take turns sitting on the eggs to keep them warm. Keeping the eggs warm is called incubation. Great horned owls incubate their eggs for four weeks. One of the adult owls must always be on the eggs to keep them warm. Sometimes a blanket of snow falls on the incubating owl, but the owl's body keeps the eggs warm.

Three-and-a-half week old owlets are being fed by their parent.

When the baby owls, called owlets, hatch, it is still winter or very early spring. With the arrival of new babies, the adult owls have to hunt for food for their offspring and themselves. Now, the winter nesting is helpful to the owls. There are no leaves, so it is easier for the owls to find prey.

Defending the nest

With babies in the nest, great horned owls become very fierce. They may try to scare enemies away by snapping their beaks, hissing, stamping their feet, and fluffing their feathers. A great horned owl in defense of its nest will spread its wings like giant fans and lift its ear tufts. A frightened great horned owl can be a very dangerous bird. Many times, great horned owls have attacked people who have strayed too close to their nests. One man remembered the great horned owl whose talons struck his head. "This was the limit," he wrote. "I did not care to be scalped or knocked to the ground." He left the nest area. For another man, "two coats, a heavy sweater, a vest, and two heavy woolen shirts" weren't enough protection. The great horned owls defending their nest clawed that man's neck and shoulder. Men wearing fur hats have been attacked, too, perhaps because the owls mistook the hat for prey.

Few animals dare to raid a great horned owl's nest. Rarely will a hawk steal an owlet. In Alaska, Indians say that black bears have climbed into great horned owls' nests and taken the young. But most predators wisely avoid the "winged tiger's" nest.

Raising great horned owlets

A great horned owl mother lays her eggs two or three days apart, so her babies hatch two or three days apart. When they break out of the eggshells, they are a little larger than baby chickens. Unlike baby chickens, which soon begin feeding themselves, great horned owl babies are helpless at birth and for some time afterward. Their eyes stay shut for a week and they cannot stand. They have a soft covering of tiny feathers known as down. The white down helps the little owls stay warm, but most of the warmth comes from their mother. The mother owl warms her babies with her feathers. As the female owl sits in the nest, the owlets rest under her wing and breast feathers. Born in February or March, the owlets may need their mother's warmth for nearly a month.

Young owls stay in the nest for six to seven weeks. During that time, the parents bring food to the owlets. When hunting is good, the adults may serve more food than the babies can eat. One great horned owl nest held eighteen pounds (8.2 kg) of dead animals!

As they grow larger, the baby owls become stronger and louder. They are no longer helpless. Their own new feathers, replacing the baby down, help them resist the cold. When someone comes near, they hiss, snap their bills, and spread their wings. The spread wings help

On the plains of Colorado, a great horned owl chick spreads its wings to look fierce.

them look larger and more fierce than they really are.

By the time the young are about forty days old, the not-so-little owls squirm out of the nest. They have become restless, and the nest seems very small to them. They stay near the nest and the adults still bring them food. The young owls can claw their way along branches, but until they begin to fly, they cannot go any great distance from the nest.

At the age of about sixty-five days, young great horned owls are ready to begin flying. Flight does not come easily. The young owls feel much safer on a perch than flapping into space. The parents help the babies

Young owls prefer sitting on a perch to flying.

overcome their fear. Instead of bringing food to the babies, the parents may perch in a nearby tree. Hunger finally drives the young owls into flight. The first few flights are for very short distances. The young owls are likely to crash land, but they are fluffy and not likely to be hurt. Afterward, they claw their way into a tree and soon try again.

Hunting skills come even more slowly than learning to fly. After a great horned owl first learns to fly, its parents still bring it food. Meanwhile, the young owl begins to fly from a perch and catch its own prey if something comes near. Its first catch may be nothing more than a plump insect. Owlets, it seems, are always hungry. Sometimes their desire to eat leads them into more distant hunting trips before the adults return.

During the summer, the young owls sharpen their skills. They fly better, and often they catch their own prey. They spend less time hooting for their parents to bring food. Meanwhile, as the young owls learn to hunt for themselves, the parents undergo a yearly change in feathers. The owls begin to lose their flight feathers, called the long wing feathers. The feathers don't all fall out at once, so the owl can still fly during this time which is called the molt. (Molting wild geese briefly lose their ability to fly.) Within a few days, each lost feather is replaced by a new one. Although the adult owls can still fly, they don't fly as well during the molt. With their young more on their own, the adults don't need to catch as much food. By late autumn the molt is complete; the adult owls have a new set of feathers.

Adult owls split up after the nesting season. Many of them rejoin each other again in late winter near the old nest. They may search for a new nesting place if there is a shortage of prey. Great horned owls are such skillful hunters that they sometimes over-hunt an area.

The young owls are on their own by November. They do not have all their adult color yet, but they are fully grown. They find and defend their own hunting territory, and no longer receive meals from their parents. Now their future depends on their own hunting ability.

In captivity, great horned owls have lived for twenty-five years. Wild birds probably don't live that long.

CHAPTER FOUR:

The range of the great horned owl

Each spring and fall, many species of birds leave on long journeys. These are migrants, birds that migrate or travel great distances from one home to another. They live in a cooler region in summer and a warmer climate in winter.

But great horned owls are not migrating birds. Most of them spend their lives fairly close to their birthplace. Great horned owls do not need to migrate. They can easily find food, and their thick feathers, right down to their toes, keep them warm.

Only the great horned owls of the Far North sometimes need to travel long distances. But even these flights are not true migrations. For one thing, the flights don't always take place. In addition, traveling great horned owls do not always end up in the same spot. They travel just far enough to find good hunting. Scientists think of true migrating birds as those which travel at a regular time and to the same place each year.

When Arctic horned owls fly south, it is because of a very hard winter. The owl's prey dies off for lack of food, and the owl is forced to leave its home.

"Home" for a great horned owl is usually just a few

"Home" for the great horned owl is just a few square miles.

square miles. But for the entire species, "home" is a huge area. Great horned owls are found throughout the United States, in Canada, Central America, and South America. They are not found in Hawaii. In the Western United States, great horned owls live in mountains nearly eleven thousand feet (3353m) above sea level. They are most often found in forests, but they can also be seen in canyons, deserts, and in the open spruce woods at the edge of the Arctic tundra.

Great horned owls are called "opportunistic" by scientists. That means that they can make the best of almost any situation in nature. They find something

Great horned owls can find a way to live in almost any area. This owl's picture was taken at Mono Lake in California.

useful in each area. They can kill and eat a wide variety of animals. One long-time owl watcher said great horned owls eat ''almost anything that moves.'' Great horned owls can nest in trees or elsewhere. Trees are the first choice, but other places will also do. Most birds cannot find opportunities in so many different kinds of living places or habitats. As a result, most birds live in a much smaller area than the great horned owl. But *Bubo*, as we have seen, is not fussy. He can find a home and ''make a living'' in many habitats.

Bubo's place in nature

Every type of animal has its place in the natural world. Each kind of animal is able to do certain things. Some animals, like mice, eat plants. Other animals are made to eat the animals that eat plants. The animals that kill and eat other animals are called predators. Foxes, wolves, mountain lions, eagles, hawks, and owls are among the predators. Hunters such as the great horned owl help keep the numbers of mice and other small animals from becoming too great.

In North America, the great horned owl is a predator in many habitats. Usually it is a predator of the forest. The forest is its favorite home. It likes to nest there, it hunts there, and it can easily hide in the forest.

While the owl hunts at night, the red-tailed hawk (left) and the peregrine falcon (right) are predators by day.

Another flying predator, the red-tailed hawk, likes the forest edges. While the owl is a night hunter, the hawk hunts in the day. By flying different "shifts,"

these two powerful hunters do not get in each other's way.

In the Far North, summer daylight lasts nearly

twenty-four hours. There, the Arctic horned owls hunt in daylight. But in other habitats, great horned owls rest during the day. They find a perch and sit, waiting for darkness. Now and then, the rest is brief. A napping owl may be discovered by a crow or another small bird, such as a blue jay. The littler bird darts around the owl and calls loudly. Soon more birds appear. All of them join in flying around the owl and calling at the top of their lungs. If the owl stays on its perch, the screaming birds will lose interest after a while. If the owl flies, the birds will follow the owl to its next perch.

Ornithologists are not sure why birds chase great horned owls or any number of other birds of prey. One thought is that the small birds view the owl as a threat to them and their nests. By calling attention to the owl, they make it less of a danger.

Mobbing birds pester the owl. They make a sleepy owl's life unpleasant. But they are no match for the owl's talons, so they don't try to hurt it. When it is fully grown, a great horned owl is very safe from other wild animals. Its curved talons and flying ability keep it quite protected. Its only real enemy is man.

Owls and man

In North America, owls have gained respect in recent years. All owls in the United States are protected by the national and state governments against killing or capture. It is even unlawful to keep an owl without a special permit. Owls, especially great horned owls, do not make good pets. Great horned owls may appear to be cuddly, feathered teddy bears, but they are not. They have been trained to hunt rabbits for falconers in years past. But they rarely, if ever, become tame, and cannot be housebroken. If someone finds an injured or orphaned owl, the bird should be turned over to an office of the United States Fish and Wildlife Service or to a wild animal rescue and recovery center.

Many centers have been started to help injured raptors, or birds of prey. People who work with these birds do not turn them into pets. They treat the bird for its injury or help it grow up. As soon as possible, they release the bird in the wild. If the bird has been badly injured, the raptor center will care for it as long as necessary. A great horned owl raised by hand is a problem for raptor centers because the bird loses its fear of humans and has not learned how to hunt. If such an owl were released, it would probably frighten someone or be killed. Or it might even starve to death.

Not many years ago, ornithologists wrote about the great horned owl's ability to do ''good'' or ''evil.'' If great horned owls ate mice and rats they were ''good.'' If they raided chicken pens they were ''evil.'' It was as if the owl, like a human being, should somehow have known right from wrong. The great horned owl, of course, is neither ''good'' nor ''bad.'' He is just an owl,

Some injured owls receive treatment at special animal centers. As soon as they are well they are released into the wild.

and he has to kill if he is going to survive. Sometimes his night hunts take him to a farm. Owls may kill ducks, chickens, pigeons, or even turkeys. Usually, though, the owl steers clear of farms unless wild prey is difficult to find. Most modern farmers know that the great horned owl kills far more mice than chickens. Still, a great horned owl risks its life when it sails into a barnyard.

The great horned owls' future

Because of people's new respect for owls, and the great horned owl's many ways of making a home for itself, *Bubo's* future in North America seems bright. No one knows how many great horned owls there are, however. With its love for deep forests and darkness, the great horned owl is impossible to count. But it seems to be holding its own, unlike a vanishing cousin, the barn owl. If we observe the laws that protect the great horned owl and save our woodlands, this raptor and its booming voice will always be part of our outdoors.

This great horned owl is shown with its young in a nest.

45

The great horned owl is
found in nearly all of
North America.

INDEX/GLOSSARY:

WILDLIFE
HABITS & HABITAT

READ AND ENJOY THE SERIES:

If you would like to know more about all kinds of wildlife, you should take a look at the other books in this series.

You'll find books on bald eagles and other birds. Books on alligators and other reptiles. There are books about deer and other big-game animals. And there are books about sharks and other creatures that live in the ocean.

In all of the books you will learn that life in the wild is not easy. But you will also learn what people can do to help wildlife survive. So read on!

DATE DUE

JAN 04			
JAN 04			
JAN 19			
APR 4			
90			